Naughty No More helped open the lines of communication. I learned so much about my son's beliefs that affect his behaviors. This book helped him to clarify and target his problems, as well as assisted in discussing positive alternatives to unwanted behaviors. After doing the activities my son proudly came home from school announcing how he made good choices just like we worked on. *Naughty No More* is full of creative activities that make learning fun. It is an amazing way to spend time with your children!

Andrea Przybylski, MS
Mental Health Counselor

"Sometimes there are adult-people who for some reason can not see your awesomeness..."

This workbook, written specifically for children, clearly displays the Mullen family's "awesomeness" and their humor in connecting with, supporting, and encouraging children to feel better about themselves. This child-centered workbook is one of those truly child-focused tools that kids can actually use, AND benefit from, AND really enjoy! The writings and activities are child-friendly, clear, fun, and warmly supportive.

With a good deal of both humor and heart, the Mullen's provide insights and suggestions for children struggling with emotions, decisions, and how to be the best 'them' they can be.

What a fabulous resource!
Kudos Andrew and Leah!

Jenn Pereira PhD, LMHC, RPT-S

This workbook engaged me from the start! I wanted to delve right in. The humor and directness spectacularly captures your attention. The activities included are practical and easy relatable. This workbook empowers children's creativity and healthy decision making skills.

Deanne (DeeDee) Ginns-Gruenberg, MA, RPT, BSN
Co-Owner of Self Esteem Shop

This book is a great tool that is valuable for families, teachers, and mental health professionals as well as students in counseling programs. The voices of the two youngest authors is both friendly and fresh.

I will be recommending this book to families in my pediatric practice.

Dr. Stuart Trust, D.O., F.A.A.P.
Clinical Professor of Pediatrics
Upstate Medical University

Naughty No
More

A workbook for children who want
to make good decisions

Andrew Mullen, Leah Mullen,
Jodi Ann Mullen, & Michael Mullen

BALBOA.
PRESS

A DIVISION OF HAY HOUSE

Balboa Press books may be ordered through booksellers or by contacting:

Balboa Press
A Division of Hay House
1663 Liberty Drive
Bloomington, IN 47403
www.balboapress.com
1-(877) 407-4847

Printed in the United States of America

ISBN: 978-1-4525-6716-7 (sc)
ISBN: 978-1-4525-6717-4 (e)

Balboa Press rev. date: 3/21/2013

Dedication

For all the kids who are good on the inside
and want to be good on the outside.

Table of Contents

Acknowledgements

(a really big and cool word for saying thanks)

We are very grateful to the people who supported and helped us with this book. A special thank you to Penny and Aaron Peter Lupo, and Andrea and Adian Przybylski who went through the entire book, and tried out the all activities testing them for the fun factor. We also appreciate June Rickli, Kid on the inside, Mental Health Counselor and Play Therapist, who helped us make this book into an opportunity to bring children together with adults that care about them.

A Letter to Parents...

Hi Parents!

First of all we would like to thank you for providing your child the opportunity to engage in this book. It is our goal to help children feel better. What we know as a family with two mental health counselors for parents and two kids who have been subjected to the special kind of strangeness that comes from being parented by counselors, is that when kids feel better they behave better (incidentally that is true for teenagers and adults too).

At eight-years-old our very own Andrew was struggling with feeling angry and stressed out. This is not typical of Andrew. However all kids, even laid back and even-tempered ones, have complex feelings. Well anyway, in his angry and stressed state Andrew decided to make a poor choice (that's as much as he wants you to know about what happened). He was found out and had to deal with the logical consequences. What impacted our family most, however, was how disappointed he was in himself.

That very same day we decided there should be a way that kids could refocus when they were about to make poor decisions and do something they would regret. That's how we developed this book. We are very proud of what we created. We think your child will enjoy the activities and feel better about him or herself as a result.

We also wanted you to know that in order for this book to help your child we need you to be willing to be invested in helping them and listening to them as they tackle the various activities. Yes, this will take up some of your time. We know you have a million things to do, the pay off is this: you will be better connected to your child. How great is that?

We would love to hear from you about your child's experience with the book and of course yours as well. It is our goal to connect adults and children in relationships based in respect and love.

One last thing Parents, if you feel like you need more help with your parenting (no one does this perfectly) check out Jodi's book, Blissful Parenting: 20 Principles for Raising Freakishly Well-Behaved & Chronically Happy Children (due out later in 2013), or listen in to our show on www.blogtalkradio.com Freakishly Well-Behaved Kids.

From our Family to Yours,

The Mullens

Introduction

Hi Kids-

We are so glad you decided to use our workbook. We hope it works for you like it works for the kids we know. You probably can do a lot of this workbook by yourself. If you get stuck or just want someone you care about to do it with you, just ask! There are grown ups all around you who want you to be the best you possible.

This workbook is for you to discover the best you possible. Sometimes there are adult-people who for some reason cannot see your awesomeness; it could be a teacher, coach, or even someone in your family. Sometimes adult-people judge you by how you act on the outside and make mistakes about the person you are on the inside. When that happens it can be hard for you and you may feel sad, angry or disappointed. In this workbook the focus is to help you feel better so you show your best self to the world. It's like magic, because when you feel better about you other people notice and may change for the better too.

You don't have to do the whole book at one time. You don't even have to do it in order. You get to decide how you want to do the activities in this book. You get to make lots of decisions in this book. You are like the boss of the book. You also are like the author, because this is really about about you. You make it up when you do the activities.

The most important things you can do to feel good on the inside and outside are to play and have fun. When you are using this workbook remember to take play breaks and have fun with the activities.

Thank you for giving our workbook a try!

Andrew, Leah, Jodi and Michael

STOP

Before you do some thing you will get in trouble for
(and feel bad about)… do this page

Some feelings are like pests, they make you want to do naughty things. They get in the way of you showing off the best you.

Put a circle around any of these feelings you have ever had….

Proud   Upset   Frustrated

Stressed   Left out   Embarrassed

Hurt   Yucky   Disappointed

Annoyed   Mad   Sad

Hey Kids: If you do not know what all these words mean find a grown-up to play feelings charades with you. It is simple: you say a feeling word on the list and the grown-up acts it out. Then you can give it a try and YOU act out the feeling word.

Pick your nose JUST KIDDING!!!!

Pick one of the feelings you circled and draw how your face looks when you have that feeling. You can show this picture to your parents or another adult who loves you so they can tell when you are feeling that feeling. You can teach your parents and other important people in your life about how you feel. You're not just the BOSS, you're also a teacher!

Time for a kid decision: Now use a different color crayon, marker or pencil to change the face you already drew to make it look like you do when you are feeling happy **or** draw another one on this page that shows what you look like when you feeling good about yourself.

Look in a mirror and make the silliest face you can. Quick go do it now. We're GLAD YOU ARE BACK. Now please draw the silly face you just made. Do you still feel a little silly? Now might be a good time to do a quick silly dance or sing a silly song. Go for it!

Change the Channel

Some times we feel bad. Some times we feel happy. On this page we want you to tell us about when you feel bad and when you feel happy. First we want you to focus on feeling bad and then change it to focus on feeling happy. It's like changing the channel from something awful on TV to something you like watching.

Now, tell us a story that starts with I feel **bad** when…

It's time for a Kid Decision: If you want to you can draw a picture too. You can do it on this page if you still have room or use another piece of paper (there are extras in the back of this book)

Tell us a story that starts with: I am **happy** when I...

It's time for a Kid Decision: If you want to you can draw a picture too. You can do it on this page if you still have room or use another piece of paper (there are extras in the back of this book).

How to Change the Channel

There are many ways you can change your FEELINGS channel. You can change your feelings channel by thinking or doing. Thinking? Yep, thinking. Think about what makes you feel good and happy. Doing? What do you do (ha that sounds like dodo) that makes you smile and feel awesome?

We will share a few of our favorites here:

Thinking:
I am powerful.
I am special.
I am a leader.
I am a good friend.

Doing:
Jumping
Spinning
Singing
Hugging

Start your own list (Did that sound bossy?):

Thinking:

Doing:

Random Scribbling Page

Flip the Switch

Ugh feeling tired stinks. It's like the energy has been zapped right out of you. You get grouchy and grumpy or just blah. On this page we want to know about times when you feel like you have only a little bit of energy. We also want to know what excites you. It's like turning on the lights in a dark room. You go from being dark and gray on the inside to lighting up with energy.

Tell us a story that starts with: My energy feels zapped when...

It's time for a Kid Decision: If you want to you can draw a picture too. You can do it on this page if you still have room or use another piece of paper (there are extras in the back of this book)

Tell us a story that starts with: I have a lot of energy when I ...

It's time for a Kid Decision: If you want to you can draw a picture too. You can do it on this page if you still have room or use another piece of paper (there are extras in the back of this book)

I'm the Boss of Me

Being the boss and in charge feels so powerful. Sometimes we let anger be the boss, but we don't have to. Below put an X next to all the times when you have let anger be the boss.

I get angry with myself when I…

- ☐ feel tired
- ☐ say things that are mean
- ☐ hurt other people
- ☐ make a mistake
- ☐ don't do well in school
- ☐ when I lose
- ☐ say things that I do not mean

You add some more…

Now try this, put an X next to the ways that you can be the boss of you even when anger is trying to be the boss.

In order to feel better I can...

- ☐ take a breath
- ☐ give myself a time out
- ☐ go for a walk (Our mom says you have to ask a grown up first)
- ☐ PLAY
- ☐ write (there are lots of pages for that in this book)
- ☐ draw
- ☐ pretend
- ☐ talk to someone

You add some...

Go "Team You!"

Being part of a team means you have people around you to support and help you. There are coaches and other players who want you to do and be your best. On this page we would like you to name all the people who are on your support team. We are going to give you some clues to help you identify these people in your life.

Your team members could be anyone. Some people who may be on your team are parents, brothers, sisters, cousins, grandparents, aunts, uncles, teachers, coaches, people at church, friend's parents, counselors, pets, friends…

Name as many as you can

"Team You" Members

♦ _____

♦ _____

♦ _____

♦ _____

♦ _____

♦ _____

- ♦ _____

- ♦ _____

- ♦ _____

- ♦ _____

- ♦ _____

There's some extra space for even more people or just to doodle or draw.
It's your decision.

"Team You" Contact Page

What do you do when you are feeling creepy and yucky and blah on the inside? Put it on the outside by talking to or playing with someone on "Team You." This page is the place to put your team members information so you can find them when you need them.

Team Member Name	Phone Number	Ok to call (if you are allowed to text you are LUCKY. Add that too.) anytime Yes or No

⇨ Remember to add new team members as you discover them!

Random Doodle Page

Dr. I.M. Gointomakeunaughty

Oh no the evil Dr. I.M. Gointomakeunaughty is at it again! This time he's trying to take over you. Who knows what tricks he has in store for you this time. Close your eyes. Can you picture what Dr. I.M. Gointomakeunaughty looks like. Quick draw him so maybe he will be easier to catch.

This is Andrew's Dr. I.M. Gointomakeunaughty

Sometimes it is hard to get a clear picture of Dr. I.M. Gointomakeunaughty. You could just write him a letter. Let him have it. Let him know you are sick of him.

Dear Dr. I.M. Gointomakeunaughty,

_____

_____

_____

_____

_____

_____

_____

_____

It's Time for a Superhero

Tell us all about the superhero that will save you from Dr. I.M. Gointomakeunaughty. Don't worry we won't tell anyone that the Superhero is you!

_____

_____

_____

_____

_____

_____

_____

What super powers will you need to defeat, conquer, and just plain win the battle against Dr. I.M. Gointomakeunaughty?

Male superhero

- ☐ Laser Vision
- ☐ Seeing into the future
- ☐ Kid talk
- ☐ Super strength on the outside
- ☐ Super strength on the inside
- ☐ Super speed
- ☐ Imagination
- ☐ Relaxation tools
- ☐ Mind reading
- ☐ Listening
- ☐ Singing silly songs
- ☐ Knock Knock Jokes

Add some more…

It Takes a lot to Defeat
Dr. I.M. Gointomakeunaughty

On this page draw the superhero that can win the fight against Dr. I.M. Gointomakeunaughty (remember you know it's you and we know it's you but Dr. I.M. Gointomakeunaughty does not, whew!) It might be a good idea for this superhero to wear a disguise.

Give your Superhero a Name: _____

Special Agent Needed

Kids everywhere need help. You need help finding out what is special about being a kid. Check off some things that are special about you. Ask a "Team You" member to look over your list to make sure you did not miss anything.

- ☐ Can pretend
- ☐ Can be silly
- ☐ Listens
- ☐ Creative problem solver
- ☐ Can be quiet
- ☐ Can be loud
- ☐ Can tell jokes
- ☐ Can blow a bubble
- ☐ Can whistle
- ☐ Can run
- ☐ Can make silly noises

- ☐ Is awesome at playing
- ☐ Uses manners
- ☐ Follows directions
- ☐ Respectful
- ☐ Can jump
- ☐ Can eat without front teeth
- ☐ Can skip
- ☐ Shares
- ☐ Reads
- ☐ Cuddles
- ☐ Gives hugs

You can add some more to the list:

Emotional Trophy Case

For this activity you may want to get the help of an adult.

An *Emotional Trophy Case* is something you get to make for yourself to look at or read when you are feeling down, sad, or alone. Really you can look at it whenever—it's your choice. You are going to create either a box to hold things in or a scrapbook for positive memories. Both can work, so you can decide what will work best for you! Yippee another **Kid Decision**!!!

Stuff you will need:
A shoe box (or any other type of smaller box you can decorate) If you have big feet it will be a big box.
Crayons, markers or colored pencils to decorate your box
Pictures from magazines or printed off the computer to decorate your box
Glue (for the pictures and photos)
Photos (ask permission to use them first otherwise someone might get mad or disappointed)
Stickers

Directions: Decorate this special box however you want, it should make you feel and think happy. Here are some ideas: Color the box, glue special pictures on it, write words that make you feel strong, put stickers on it, or find a picture of a trophy and put that on the box.

(This can be done with a scrapbook as well.)

What to put in the box:

Once you have the box decorated your special way, you can put anything in it that makes you feel good about yourself. Here is a list of things you can start with:

Any trophy or medals you have won or earned

Any awards you have received

Any certificates you have gotten

Any cards or notes people have given you that make you feel special

Any pictures that make you laugh or feel good inside (the pictures can be of you or of other people that make you feel special or even pictures of you and other people)

Pictures of your pets, family, friends

Any pictures you have drawn that you are proud of

Any report cards, tests or school projects you feel proud about

Now what?

What to do with the box once you have some things in it:

Keep your box in a safe place where you can get to it. Take it out anytime you want. The box reminds you how special you really are and there are people who love you and think you are special too.

You can use the next page to write down or draw some of the things you want to include in your Emotional Trophy Case.

Feelings Word Search

Directions: Find the feeling words in the box. When you find the feeling word make a face that shows what it looks like when you have that feeling.

D	Q	F	L	M	E	X	C	I	T	E	D
B	O	D	M	A	N	C	O	S	K	R	P
C	Z	S	A	D	V	N	S	U	B	J	C
R	U	G	A	N	G	R	Y	H	N	W	O
X	E	R	P	A	T	I	E	N	T	X	N
S	X	L	I	U	D	N	H	P	U	G	F
I	C	J	A	O	S	Z	A	X	C	L	U
L	B	G	K	X	U	F	P	E	U	B	S
L	L	R	U	M	E	S	P	F	R	L	E
Y	A	C	O	V	T	D	Y	T	I	J	D
E	S	B	A	N	N	O	Y	E	D	P	X
D	G	I	L	O	J	C	U	R	I	M	E

Angry	Joyful
Annoyed	Mad
Confused	Patient
Curious	Relaxed
Excited	Sad
Happy	Silly

Magical Foods

Some foods actually can change your rotten mood to a magical mood—we know because we have tried this out. Yum! Our Mom and Dad keep an eye on us, or even join us when we do this and make us clean up too!

Oranges: Oranges are sweet juicy and also can be silly!

Try this: Ask a grown up to cut an orange into four slices. Put a slice with the skin facing out in your mouth. Then give a BIG smile! You will get a cool new look for your teeth!

Have you ever eaten a rainbow? Having a rainbow inside of you would feel magical!

Peppers are come in all different colors. Have a grown up help you cut the peppers into strips and then eat your way through the colors of the rainbow! Can you think of other rainbow foods that are created in nature?

RAINBOW FRUIT SALAD:
RED- Strawberries, apples, or raspberries
ORANGE- Oranges, peaches, mango
YELLOW- Pineapple, bananas
GREEN- Kiwi, green grapes, green apple
BLUE- Blueberries
INDIGO/PURPLE- Blackberries, plums

Grapes: Grapes are fun to eat. They have a funky taste in between sweet and sour!

Try this: Put two grapes in between your teeth and your cheeks. Now put your hands on your cheeks and... SQUEEZE! What happens? Clue: Have napkins ready. *This also works really well with cherry tomatoes! (Our Mom is an expert at this).

Bananas: They are sweet, squishy, and YUMMY!

Here is a way to make a healthy banana treat we call Monkey Poop!

To make Monkey Poop: Mush together ripe bananas, a splash of vanilla extract, a pinch of cinnamon, a dash of sugar, chocolate chips, and a squirt of chocolate syrup. Then put the mixture in the freezer. Wait an hour. If you really want to freak your parents out take the hour to help with chores or read! Make sure you have a grown up help you make your Monkey Poop. Oh, and never eat real poop.

Apples: Apples can be sweet, tart or somewhere in between. They are crunchy too.

Try this: Ask an adult to cut the apple sideways. Then look inside. What do the seeds look like? Here's a hint: Twinkle twinkle little _____. Can you imagine this being inside of you too?

TIP: Watch out for holes! If the apple you are eating has a hole in it there may be a worm inside. Unless you want to eat a worm then don't worry about the holes! Yuck!

*Now tell us some of your favorite foods that are good for you on the outside and make you feel good on the inside!

Be a Detective

Kids like you are great most of the time. Sometimes it is hard to tell if you are choosing to behave or be naughty. It's times like this that you can use a detective. This top-secret detective knows what clues to look for when it comes to having excellent behavior.

Our detective has found some clues. Help the detective figure out which clues are for the awesomely behaved kid, and which behaviors were poor choices that lead adults to think the kid is naughty or bad. Circle the word good or naughty next to each clue to show that you have top-notch detective skills too.

Here are the clues the detective has found:

Helping someone, just because.   Good or Naughty?

Talking back to your mom or dad.   Good or Naughty?

Hitting a person.   Good or Naughty?

Making your bed without being asked.   Good or Naughty?

Helping your family in the kitchen.   Good or Naughty?

Making fun of your sister, brother or friend.   Good or Naughty?

Taking something that does not belong to you.   Good or Naughty?

Telling a friend something you like about him or her. Good or Naughty?

Lying so you don't get in trouble.   Good or Naughty?

HOORAY!!!! You know what to look for.

You can find clues anywhere. Just watch people do stuff. Watch your friends, teachers, parents, and even watch yourself. Turn on your detective skills. What clues have you found?

What are some clues that show good choices?

What are examples or clues that people made poor behavior choices?

What clues do you leave behind to show YOU know how to make good behavior choices?

Celebrate You!

Don't you think it's about time to have a party? Well we do! We want to have a party to celebrate you! Nobody is like you. You are special and unique in your own way!

Share with us what you think is great about you. On this page we want you to write what you love about yourself and what makes you special. Are you an awesome soccer player? Are you super smart? Can you sing like an angel? Tell us everything you think is cool about you. Tell us about what's special about you on the inside and outside.

You can list all your awesome traits here:

Magic Mirror

Sometimes we all feel like we can't do anything right. We try and we try, but things just don't go our way. When things like this happen it makes us want to give up trying. We feel like quitting. Giving up never works. We end up feeling worse. The Magic Mirror can help when you are feeling this way, and it is easy to do. All you need is a quiet place and a mirror.

How to use the Magic Mirror:

1. Once you have a quiet place and a mirror, you start by looking at yourself in the mirror.

2. While you are looking at yourself you will start to talk to yourself. Trust us, even though this sounds weird everyone talks to themselves sometimes. We catch our Mom and Dad talking to themselves all the time!

That's it! "Hold on. What should I say to myself?"

Good question! What you want to say to yourself is anything positive about yourself.

Here are some examples:

- I am strong!
- I never quit!
- I love myself, even when I make mistakes!
- I am a unique person!
- I CAN DO IT!

Now add a few things you think you can say to yourself here:

Work at doing this at least once a day for a week straight, and you'll find you will start becoming a happier person. Do it everyday for one whole month to make sure the magic takes effect.

Rain, Rain, Go Away

Everyone gets upset. When you're upset it feels like a rainy day on the inside. You get feeling, thinking, and acting like the sun will never come out. This page is all about how to bring some sunshine to your inner rainy day.

The rainbow project:

If you are feeling upset and can't seem to let your sunshine through the dark clouds- do this!

1. Make a list of all the things that make you happy.

2. Get a nice piece of paper. Poster board will work too.

3. Write all the things that make you happy down on the paper. Don't forget to use lots of color! Just like the rainbow.

Now whenever you are feeling sad or upset inside look at your rainbow and do one of the things that make you happy. One of the things that will turn your day from gray and cloudy, to colorful and fun!

One More Thing

Being your best self is hard work. It takes practice. We know you can do it. You have to believe you can do it too. Even though this is the end of the book, it is really the beginning of you feeling proud and good about you. When you feel proud and good about you, other people will feel that way about you too.

Let us know how you are doing! You can email us at naughtynomore@gmail.com or write us a letter or send a drawing to: Naughty No More at Integrative Counseling Services, 5 West Cayuga St, Oswego NY 13126.

About the Authors

Andrew-is 9-years-old and loves the family's two cats. He enjoys playing basketball, football, soccer, and lacrosse. He also enjoys reading. Andrew thinks he may either want to be an engineer or make special effects in movies. One random thing about Andrew is: His favorite video game is "Pokémon Black."

Leah-is 13-years-old. She enjoys writing, figure skating, dance, jewelry making, singing and acting. Leah wants to be an actress, chef, or author when she grows up (Hey- She's an author NOW). She describes herself as funny, nice, silly, and a little weird. One random thing about Leah is: She can drive a golf cart.

Jodi-is a professor, counselor, author, parent coach, and play therapist. For work, she gets to play with kids to help them feel better. She likes to play outside. One random thing about Jodi is: She can't pronounce the word "acorn" (She says "Egghorn").

Michael- is also a counselor and professor. He does consulting work for businesses and coaches professionals. He has also coached high school and college basketball, and currently works coaching in youth sports. One random thing about Michael is: When he was in fifth grade he had his front tooth knocked out playing football!

Printed in the United States
By Bookmasters